THE VIKINGS

AT A GLANCE

MIKE CORBISHLEY

PETER BEDRICK BOOKS

NEW YORK

Published by
PETER BEDRICK BOOKS
156 Fifth Avenue
New York, NY 10010

© Macdonald Young Books 1998
Text and illustrations © Macdonald Young Books

The right of Mike Corbishley to be identified as the Author
of this Work has been asserted by him in accordance with the
Copyright, Designs and Patents Act 1988.

Edited by: Annie Scothern
Series edited by: Lisa Edwards
Designed by: The Design Works, Reading, UK
Illustrated by: Maltings Partnership
Consultant: Dr. Julian Richards, University of York
Runic consultant: Dr. Judith Jesch

Library of Congress Cataloging-in-Publication Data
Corbishley, Mike.
The Vikings / Mike Corbishley.
p. cm. -- (At a glance)
Includes index.
Summary: An illustrated survey of the history, politics,
culture, and daily life of the Vikings.
ISBN 0-87226-558-7 (alk. paper)
1. Vikings--Juvenile literature. [1.Vikings.] I. Title.
II. Series.
DL65.C67 1998
948'. 022--dc21 98-12939
CIP
AC

Printed in Hong Kong by Wing King Tong
First American edition, 1998

CONTENTS

Time Track

The Vikings sailed from Scandinavia (the countries we now call Norway, Sweden and Denmark) to many lands, in some cases being the first people to settle there and farm. Sometimes the Vikings took the place of invaders who had come before.

The first kingdoms in Scandinavia were probably established between 600 and 800. But by about 1100 the Viking age was over in most areas, although descendants of the Vikings still ruled in different parts of the world. ▼

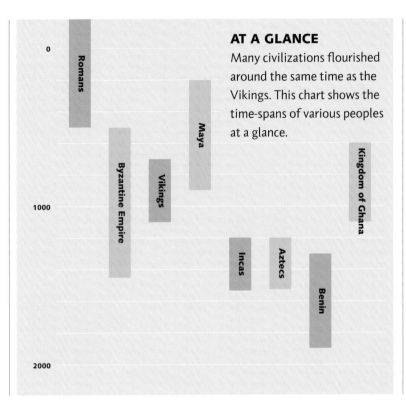

AT A GLANCE
Many civilizations flourished around the same time as the Vikings. This chart shows the time-spans of various peoples at a glance.

Chart labels: Romans, Maya, Byzantine Empire, Vikings, Kingdom of Ghana, Incas, Aztecs, Benin

Chart scale: 0, 1000, 2000

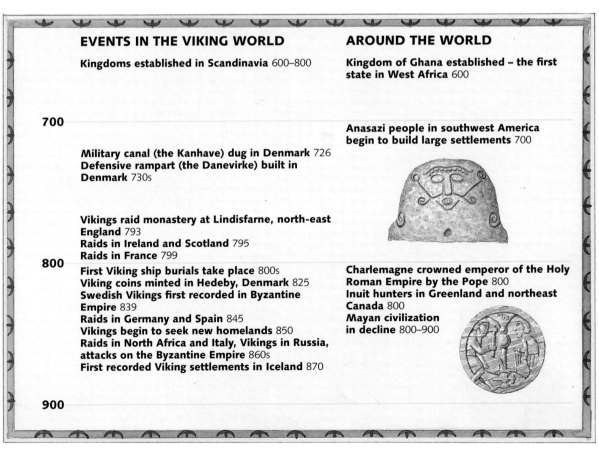

EVENTS IN THE VIKING WORLD

Kingdoms established in Scandinavia 600–800

700

Military canal (the Kanhave) dug in Denmark 726
Defensive rampart (the Danevirke) built in Denmark 730s

Vikings raid monastery at Lindisfarne, north-east England 793
Raids in Ireland and Scotland 795
Raids in France 799

800
First Viking ship burials take place 800s
Viking coins minted in Hedeby, Denmark 825
Swedish Vikings first recorded in Byzantine Empire 839
Raids in Germany and Spain 845
Vikings begin to seek new homelands 850
Raids in North Africa and Italy, Vikings in Russia, attacks on the Byzantine Empire 860s
First recorded Viking settlements in Iceland 870

900

AROUND THE WORLD

Kingdom of Ghana established – the first state in West Africa 600

Anasazi people in southwest America begin to build large settlements 700

Charlemagne crowned emperor of the Holy Roman Empire by the Pope 800
Inuit hunters in Greenland and northeast Canada 800
Mayan civilization in decline 800–900

EVENTS IN THE VIKING WORLD	AROUND THE WORLD

900

Vikings given Normandy in France 911
Vikings begin to occupy Brittany in France 914
Viking republic established in Iceland 930

Birth of Quetzalcoatl, considered a god by the Aztecs 947
Christianity spreads through Russia 957

Eric Bloodaxe is killed 954
Harald Bluetooth converts the Danes to Christianity c.965
Round forts built in Denmark c.980
New raids on England 980s
Vikings in Greenland 985

1000

Viking voyages to North America c.1000
Brian Boru, the king of the Irish, defeats the Vikings in battle 1014
Cnut is the king of England 1016–35
First stone church built in Denmark 1027
Death of Harthacnut (Cnut's son), the last Viking king of England 1042
English defeat Norwegian Vikings at the Battle of Stamford Bridge 1066

New Zealand first settled 1000

Muslim conquest of West Africa 1054

First western Christian crusade against the Muslims in the Holy Land 1096

1100

The Norwegian king, Sigurd the Jerusalem-farer, leads a crusade to the Holy Land 1107

Paper-making spreads into Europe from the Muslim Empire 1150
University of Paris is founded 1150

Saladin, the Muslim leader, recaptures Jerusalem 1187

1200

Beginnings of Aztec power 1200
Arabic numerals introduced into Europe 1202
Genghis Khan leads Mongol invasion of China 1211

Greenland is ruled directly from Norway 1261
Iceland is ruled directly from Norway 1263

Marco Polo arrives in China from Venice, Italy 1275

1300

The Inuit begin to occupy Greenland 1341

The Black Death plague begins in Asia c.1341

The Portuguese reach the Canary Islands, off the west coast of Africa 1397

1400

Last Norwegian colony in Greenland 1400s

Bartolomeu Diaz sails around the Cape of Good Hope in southern Africa 1487

SITE-SEEING – A GUIDE TO THE VIKING WORLD

The name 'Viking' probably comes from the word *vikingr* in the Old Norse language. This word meant a pirate or a raider from Scandinavia. Many people were terrified of the Vikings, calling them 'heathens' or 'wolves to be feared.' The Vikings were famous travelers of the ancient world. In their warships they sailed across their known world, and then beyond it. Some voyages were to plunder other people's lands, but some were in search of new lands where the Vikings could settle.

The Vikings were also great traders, reaching as far as Constantinople (now called Istanbul) in Turkey. We know that they even got as far as North America eventually, by way of Iceland and Greenland.

Vinland

We are told that around the year 1000 Leif Eriksson set out from Greenland to find a land that had been reported by another Viking traveler. Eriksson discovered wild grapes on vines here and so he called the land Vinland. The Vikings had landed in North America.

Greenland

The first Vikings came to this ice-bound island sometime in the tenth century. Erik the Red made his second voyage here in 985 and built some settlements.

Ireland

This country was raided by the Vikings from 795. Nearly fifty years later, the Vikings had built fortresses and permanent settlements. Dublin was originally a Viking town.

Scotland

By the ninth century, Vikings from Norway had begun to settle on the Shetland Islands, the Orkneys and the Hebrides. Then they moved down the west coast of Scotland to Ireland.

England

The first raid on England was probably in 793, when the Vikings raided the monastery at Lindisfarne. Over the next fifty years or so, the Vikings raided and invaded the whole eastern coast of England.

Jorvik

The Vikings attacked the town of Eoforwic in northeast England on November 1, 866. In 875 they came back to settle here. Renamed Jorvik, the town soon became an important center for trade and crafts.

Iceland
Gardar the Swede was probably the first Viking to reach Iceland in about 860. Settlers arrived on Iceland around ten years later.

Hedeby
The Viking town of Hedeby was founded in the eighth century as a trading port. Its workshops made fine objects from bone and metal for export.

Trelleborg
In some places the Vikings built forts. One fort was at Trelleborg in Denmark. A huge circular mound of earth and wood defended it. Inside there were workshops and buildings for families.

ORKNEY ISLANDS
HEBRIDES
SHETLAND ISLANDS
NORWAY
SWEDEN
FINLAND
RUSSIA
SCOTLAND
NORTH SEA
Lindisfarne
DENMARK
Dublin
Jorvik (York)
Trelleborg
IRELAND
Hedeby
ENGLAND
Paris
FRANCE
BLACK SEA
ITALY
Constantinople
PORTUGAL
SPAIN
TURKEY
STRAIT OF GIBRALTAR
MEDITERRANEAN SEA

France
The coast of France was raided many times by the Vikings. In 911 the king of the Franks gave part of his lands to the Vikings. An army, led by Rollo the Viking, was brought in to keep other Vikings from invading the kingdom around Paris.

The Mediterranean lands
From a base in western France, around 100 Viking ships began to raid the coastal areas of the countries we now know as Portugal and Spain. By the year 860 the Vikings had sailed through the Strait of Gibraltar and attacked Italy.

The East
Vikings from Sweden sailed into Russia along its great rivers. It is thought that these Vikings were known as the Rus, which is how Russia got its name. Their reason for travelling was to trade furs for silk, spices and silver. The Vikings even reached and attacked Constantinople – the capital of the Byzantine Empire.

HOMELANDS OF THE VIKINGS

In the eighth and ninth centuries, Scandinavian people from Norway, Sweden and Denmark who went on expeditions abroad were said to have gone 'a-viking.' Over the years, the term 'Viking' has come to mean anyone who lived in Scandinavia during the Viking age (700–1100). Surrounded by sea, Scandinavia has many different regions – from good farming land in the south and east to high mountains, dense forests and deep lakes further north. In their homelands, the Vikings were farmers, town builders and great traders. ▼

Coin from Hedeby showing a Viking warship with a sail and row of shields.

SEARCHING FOR NEW LANDS

Although most Vikings stayed in their homelands, many went in search of new lands. Sometimes these Vikings traveled to find better land to farm; sometimes they went to plunder so that they could return to their homelands as wealthy men. The Vikings were used to traveling locally by ship – along the coasts and on the rivers. But as time went on, Viking adventurers sailed further and further westwards.

VIKING TOWNS

Hedeby, was an important Viking town. It was a market town with a harbor, and was one of the first towns in Scandinavia to mint coins. All sorts of crafts and trades made the town wealthy and important – ships were repaired in the harbor, pots and glassware were made in the workshops, and bone and amber were carved into everyday objects and jewelry. The town was planned. Many of the streets were paved with logs, and laid out straight and at right angles to each other. The houses faced on to the streets and were made from wooden planks.

A FARMING VILLAGE

In Denmark, a Viking farming village called Vorbasse has been excavated by archeologists. From around 700 to 1000 there were seven farms in the village, each with its own longhouse, barns and workshops. Each farm kept about twenty cows and also grew grain for flour.

KEY

1 longhouse
2 barns
3 workshops
4 grain crops – wheat, barley or rye
5 wooden enclosure around each farm

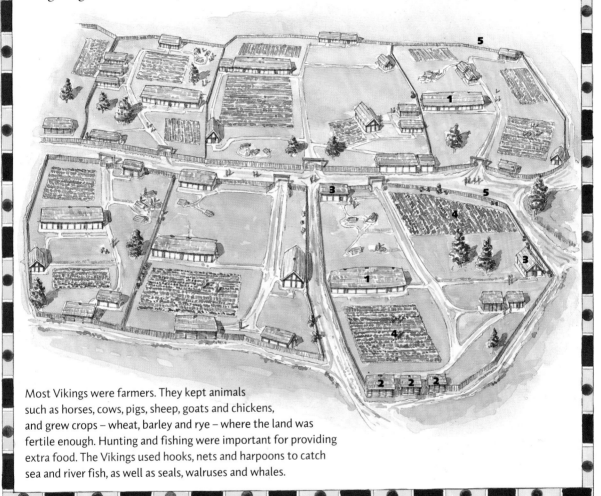

Most Vikings were farmers. They kept animals such as horses, cows, pigs, sheep, goats and chickens, and grew crops – wheat, barley and rye – where the land was fertile enough. Hunting and fishing were important for providing extra food. The Vikings used hooks, nets and harpoons to catch sea and river fish, as well as seals, walruses and whales.

REACHING AMERICA

Viking settlers reached the continent of North America 500 years before Christopher Columbus arrived there. Cargo ships carried people, goods and animals vast distances from the Viking homelands, gradually advancing further west. Erik the Red reached a land near to America. It was ice-bound and had very little land that could be farmed. But he wanted to attract settlers there so he called it Greenland. Vikings reached America around the year 1000 and named the place where they landed 'Vinland.' It was probably Newfoundland as archeologists have found objects in Newfoundland that may have come from Norway.

This Viking ship, called a *knarr*, was used by traders and settlers.

TRADE AND TRANSPORT

The Vikings probably traveled further than any other ancient peoples. They journeyed to other lands to settle, plunder or trade. In their homelands the Vikings had a number of goods and materials that they could use for trade with other countries. Forests provided timber; iron ore could be dug up and smelted to make weapons and tools; amber, animal bones and ivory from walruses could all be carved. The Vikings traveled east to the Black Sea and then beyond the Caspian Sea to find goods in exchange. They were looking for silk and spices but especially for silver. Before coins were used, some silver objects (often jewelry) were chopped up and used for exchange. ▼

A TRADE IN SLAVES ▲
The Vikings also bought and sold slaves. Some slaves were taken back to Scandinavia to work on farms or in towns. Others were sold on, especially in exchange for silver in Arab countries.

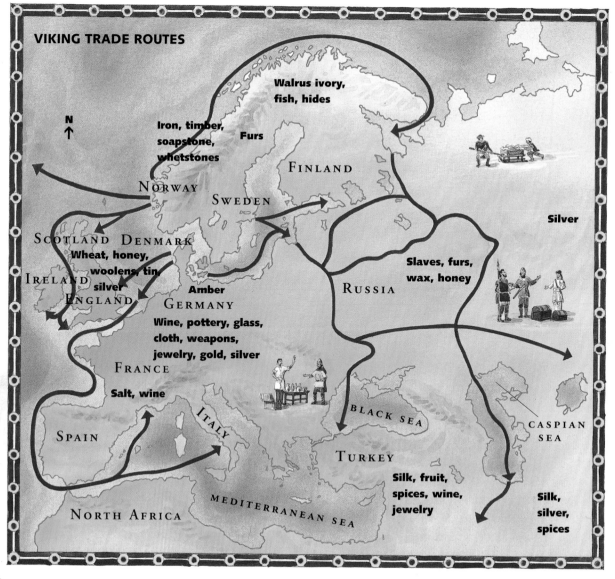

VIKING TRADE ROUTES

N ↑

Walrus ivory, fish, hides

Iron, timber, soapstone, whetstones

Furs

FINLAND

NORWAY

SWEDEN

Silver

SCOTLAND DENMARK

Wheat, honey, woolens, tin, silver

IRELAND

ENGLAND

Amber

GERMANY

Slaves, furs, wax, honey

RUSSIA

Wine, pottery, glass, cloth, weapons, jewelry, gold, silver

FRANCE

Salt, wine

ITALY

BLACK SEA

CASPIAN SEA

SPAIN

TURKEY

Silk, fruit, spices, wine, jewelry

Silk, silver, spices

NORTH AFRICA

MEDITERRANEAN SEA

TRAVELING OVERLAND

Most Viking journeys were made on water, either on rivers or on the sea. But the Vikings did travel on land as well. Some of them rode on horseback. Goods were transported in wagons or on sledges in winter. There were some specially built roads in the Viking homelands such as causeways over marshy land, built from logs or brushwood or even packed gravel or stone.

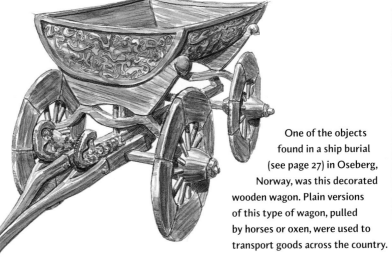

One of the objects found in a ship burial (see page 27) in Oseberg, Norway, was this decorated wooden wagon. Plain versions of this type of wagon, pulled by horses or oxen, were used to transport goods across the country.

OVER THE ICE

Some of the Viking homelands were covered with snow and ice for part or all of the year. So skating over frozen lakes and rivers was a common way of getting around. People traveled in ice-sledges pulled by horses, or they used ice-skates. Skaters used a pole to push down on to the ice to pick up speed.

▲ The blade of this ice-skate is an animal bone that has been highly polished on the underneath edge. It would have been tied to the leather ankle-boot with strips of leather.

Kings and Things

From the beginning of the ninth century, some Scandinavian countries had their own kings. The king was the most important ruler, but there were others in the country who also held power. Assemblies of the people could make decisions too.

Who held power?

The king was the most important ruler.

Below the king were the nobles. The highest ranking noble was called a chieftain, or *jarl*. He had his own band of warriors. Jarls often led Viking raids on other countries.

The chieftains ruled over the freemen, called *karlars*. Most freemen were farmers. Specialists such as shipwrights and metal workers were freemen too.

Slaves, or *thralls*, could be bought or sold. They were not free people, but they could be set free by their master.

A Famous Viking

Eric Bloodaxe had a reputation as a fierce warrior, as his name implies. He was the king of Norway from 930 to about 936, when he was driven off the throne by his younger brother, Hakon the Good. Eric went into exile and became the king of York between 948 and 954. He was eventually driven out of York and killed in an ambush. His coin reads ERIC REX – *rex* is Latin for 'king.'

Making the rules

Freemen had the right to carry weapons and to take part in the district assembly, called the *thing*. At these assemblies laws were read out and decisions were made. Disputes could be discussed. People who did not obey the laws became outlaws, or *nithings*. Outlaws had to give up their possessions and leave the country. In Iceland, which did not have a king, all matters were discussed in a type of parliament called an *althing*. This assembly of all the freemen of Iceland met for two weeks at midsummer each year at a place called Thingvellir. Although only freemen could vote, families came along as well to buy at stalls that were set up there during the assembly.

THE JELLING STONE

Harald Bluetooth was the king of Denmark from around 958 to 987. When he converted to Christianity in 965, he built a church next to his father's burial mound at a place called Jelling. Then he put up a memorial stone – the greatest Viking monument in Scandinavia – to honor his parents. The stone has three carved sides.

KEY

1 this side shows a great beast with claws and a long curling tail

2 a snake is entwined around the beast

3 the next side has Christ at its center

4 intertwining ribbons wrap around the figure of Christ

5 the third side has an inscription that continues on the other sides

6 the stone is decorated with an intertwining border pattern

The inscription reads: 'King Harald ordered this memorial to be made in memory of Gorm, his father, and in memory of Thyre, his mother – that was the Harald who won for himself all Denmark and Norway, and made the Danes Christians.'

VICTORIOUS VIKINGS

Gardar the Swede is the first Viking to reach Iceland c.860

900

Rollo the Viking is made Count of Normandy by the king of France 911

Eric Bloodaxe is the king of Norway 930–36
Hakon the Good throws Eric Bloodaxe out of Norway and becomes the first Christian king of Norway 936
Eric Bloodaxe is the king of York 948–54
Harald Bluetooth becomes the king of Denmark 958

1000

Leif Eriksson arrives in Vinland (now Newfoundland) c.1000
Cnut becomes the first Viking king of England 1016
Cnut becomes the king of Denmark as well as the king of England 1019
Harthacnut becomes the last Viking king of England 1035

Carved chess pieces from the twelfth century showing a king and his court

1100

The Norwegian king, Sigurd the Jerusalem-farer, leads a crusade to the Holy Land 1107

Viking Society

The idea of 'family' was very important to the Vikings. Most people lived in large families, which included aunts, uncles, nephews, nieces and grandparents as well as parents and children. Family houses were usually crowded as there were sometimes slaves too! Loyalty to the family, before anyone else, was most important. It was the duty of the man, the master of the family, to protect his extended family and to keep a good name and reputation for them all.

SPINNING

A spindle is a wooden rod shaped like this: ▼

A spindle whorl is a piece of clay or bone that fits on to the spindle. Its weight causes the spindle to turn. As the spindle turns (spins), it stretches the wool or flax into yarn (thread).

VIKING WOMEN

Most Viking women worked in the home, preparing the meals, looking after the children, making clothes and looking after the animals. Viking men did the heavy farm work, or hunted and fished, or traded and fought. There were no women warriors, although some women did go with their husbands to battles and then settle in newly conquered lands. Women were not allowed to take part in public life, but they made major decisions in the home and were responsible for other members of the family and slaves. A woman would run the farm or business if her husband was away.

KEY

1 a spindle and spindle whorl

2 a loom for weaving the yarn into cloth

3 weights to keep the yarn stretched tight

4 metal cauldron in which stews of meat and vegetables were cooked

5 fork for roasting meat over the fire

6 wooden bowls, plates and spoons (the Vikings did not use forks for eating)

7 wooden bucket and ladle

8 clay cooking pot

9 *quern* for grinding barley into flour for bread

10 wooden trough for kneading dough to make bread

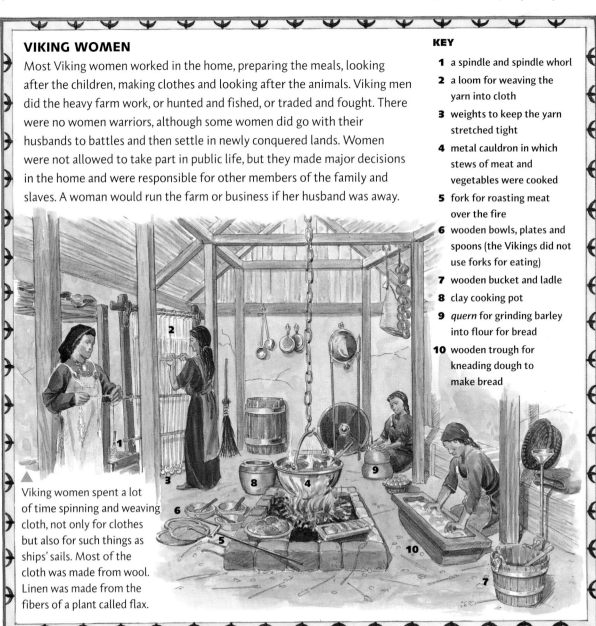

Viking women spent a lot of time spinning and weaving cloth, not only for clothes but also for such things as ships' sails. Most of the cloth was made from wool. Linen was made from the fibers of a plant called flax.

VIKING CRAFTS

In all Viking towns you would have seen a great variety of things being made in workshops along the streets by craftsmen such as wood turners, leather workers or bone carvers. People practicing the same craft sometimes built their workshops in the same part of town.

CHILDREN

When a baby was born, the parents sprinkled water over the child and chose a name. The Vikings did not use surnames, as we do today. They used the father's name or adapted it – Leif, son of Erik, or Leif Eriksson. Viking children did not go to school. They helped their parents from about seven years old. Boys might work in the fields or in the workshop. Girls might help with the animals or learn how to weave.

THE LAW

Crimes and disputes between people were discussed at assemblies called *things*. Panels of neighbors were brought together to call witnesses and to decide on the penalty. Common thieves could be hanged but the general penalty for crimes was payment of a fine. Even if someone was found guilty of manslaughter, the penalty was a fine called a *wergild*, meaning 'man-value.' Sometimes disputes between families turned into feuds. It was then a family duty to kill someone in the murderer's family. Blood-feuds often lasted for generations.

MONEY

For a long time the Vikings did not use coins to pay for things. They had two methods of payment. One was to barter – swapping goods of the same value. The other was to use silver by weight to pay for goods. Merchants used portable scales to weigh the silver, often cutting up jewelry or coins taken from other countries. From the ninth century the Vikings started to make their own coins, copying designs from coins made by other people they came into contact with.

Everyday Life

Viking houses were busy, noisy places. The Vikings liked to entertain themselves and their guests. On cold winter evenings, families might sing and dance, play board games or listen to stories. You might think the Vikings must have been dirty people – working in the fields or in workshops, or cooking and weaving inside smoky houses. But the Vikings washed and took care of their appearance.

Vikings had combs made out of antler or bone to keep hair, mustaches and beards tidy.

HOUSES

The most important part of a Viking house was the large living room, which was used for sleeping as well as eating. It was in the center of the house and had an open fireplace, or hearth, in the middle. The smoke from the fire drifted up into the roof and out through a smoke hole.

Wrapped in rugs and animal furs, people slept on raised platforms around the walls. Those who could afford to might have had mattresses and pillows filled with chicken feathers or down from ducks.

There were very few pieces of furniture in Viking houses – perhaps only chests to store clothes in.

The Vikings liked to be hospitable to their guests and prepared large quantities of food and drink for them.

The Vikings loved listening to stories, especially legends about great events in the past. Poets called *skalds* traveled the country reciting their verse at feasts or for after-dinner entertainment.

MUSIC AND GAMES

Music was played on flutes or pipes made from the hollow bones of animals – a sheep's leg bone or the wing bone of a goose or swan.

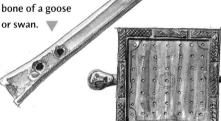

The Vikings liked playing games, especially board games. It is thought that they brought back the idea of chess from Arabia.

Board from the Viking game called *hneftafl*. One player used eight pieces to protect the king from the other player, who had sixteen pieces.

CLOTHES

Viking clothes can look simple, even strange to us today. But those who could afford to wore decorated, colorful clothes and both men and women wore jewelry. Most of the clothes were made at home from wool or linen. The rich could buy more expensive materials, such as silk. These were imported from the East by merchants.

FOOD AND DRINK

Viking families ate the main meal of the day in the evening after work. What you had to eat depended on how rich or poor you were. But there was a great variety of foods to choose from, if you could get them.

Viking farmers grew barley and rye for bread and porridge. Bread was baked on the hearth or in special ovens in richer houses.

There was meat from sheep, cows, pigs, goats and even horses.

The most usual vegetables were peas, onions, garlic and cabbages.

Eggs from chickens, ducks, geese and seabirds were eaten.

Some foods, such as fish, were dried or pickled to preserve them.

Salt, horseradish, mustard, dill, coriander and rarer spices brought from the East, such as cumin, were used to flavor food.

Men hunted for hares, deer and wild boar and fished wherever they could.

The Vikings drank milk as well as making it into butter and cheese. But they were most famous for their beer. Women brewed the beer from malted barley. Beer was used for everyday drinking, feasts and parties. Different fruits and honeys were also available at various times of the year. Sometimes these were made into alcoholic drinks.

Beer was often drunk in huge quantities from cattle horns.

KEY

1 a woman wore a long linen dress

2 a woolen tunic like an apron

3 brooches to fasten the tunic

4 a shawl and fastening brooch

5 finger rings

6 necklaces

7 leather shoes

8 a man wore trousers held up by a sash or drawstring

9 a tunic and belt

10 a heavy cloak in winter

11 a brooch to fasten the cloak

12 leather shoes or ankle boots

WARRIORS AND RAIDERS

Viking raiders were regarded by their enemies as 'wolves to be feared' and 'ruthless, angry, foreign, purely pagan people.' But how did the Vikings see themselves? To go *I viking* ('a-viking') meant to go on an expedition to get wealth and honor. A Viking warrior thought that fighting battles brought glory for himself and his family.

BODY PROTECTION

Shields were made of wood – painted in bright colors – with a metal 'boss' to protect the hand grip.

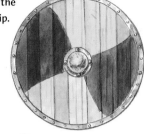

Helmets often had protective strips for the nose or eye pieces, and chain-mail to protect the neck.

Heavy chain-mail shirts were made from thousands of iron rings.

Tunics of padded leather stopped cuts from swords.

WARRIORS 'A-VIKING'

Viking warriors did not wear a standard uniform like soldiers in armies today, but this is what some of the warriors looked like. A warrior was protected by body armor and carried a variety of weapons.

WEAPONS

All free Viking men had the right to carry weapons, even at home. The main weapons were a sword, a spear, a dagger and an axe.

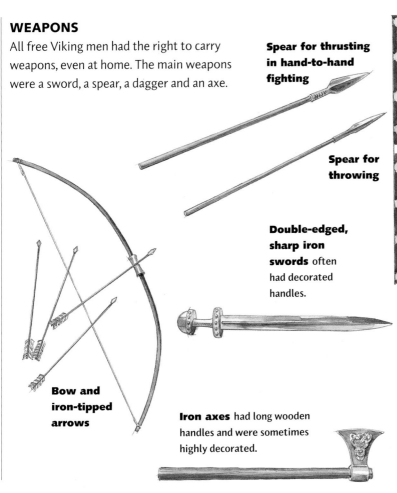

Spear for thrusting in hand-to-hand fighting

Spear for throwing

Double-edged, sharp iron swords often had decorated handles.

Bow and iron-tipped arrows

Iron axes had long wooden handles and were sometimes highly decorated.

An Arab traveler who came across Viking warriors in Russia wrote this about them: *'They have huge bodies and great courage. Each warrior usually carries with him some craftsman's tools such as an axe. He fights on foot with a spear and a shield. He carries a sword and dagger and has a throwing spear slung across his back.'*

VIKING FORTS

The Vikings built a number of large forts in Denmark during the reign of Harald Bluetooth. Each fort was protected by huge ramparts of earth – with timbers to strengthen them – and deep ditches. The inside of the fort was divided into quarters by roads. The roads led to four wooden gateways. Each quarter of the fort had long houses arranged in a square. It was not just warriors who lived in the forts. Archeologists have also found the bones of women and children. It is thought that the forts may have been used as centers for the local collection of taxes.

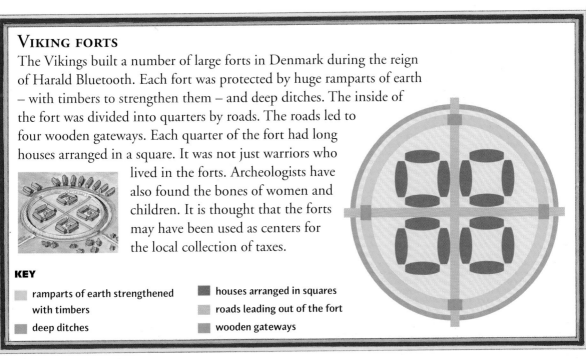

KEY

- ramparts of earth strengthened with timbers
- deep ditches
- houses arranged in squares
- roads leading out of the fort
- wooden gateways

VIKING BUILDERS

The Vikings were excellent craftspeople, using a variety of materials to make everyday objects, weapons and jewelry. But it was the carpenters who produced the most impressive Viking constructions – buildings and ships made of wood. These skillful woodworkers knew how to cut huge trees into planks of just the right size and shape, and how to carve elaborate designs on panels or on the prows of warships.

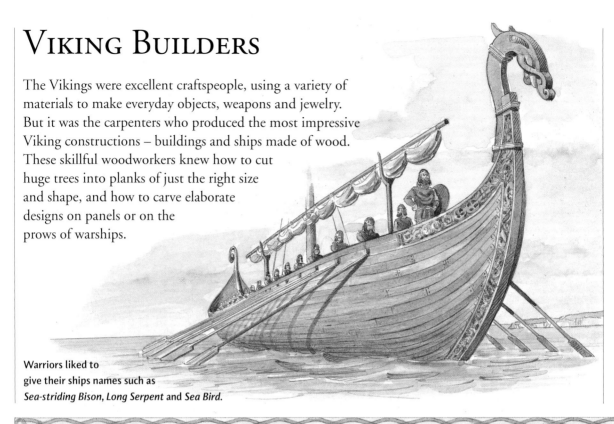

Warriors liked to give their ships names such as *Sea-striding Bison, Long Serpent* and *Sea Bird*.

BUILDING A VIKING SHIP

Specialist carpenters (shipwrights) built Viking ships in the open as near to the water as possible. These shipwrights did not work from drawn plans but from knowledge and experience handed down from generation to generation. Warships were the largest ships they built. The longest Viking ship ever found measures 92 feet.

1 Shipwrights made the 'backbone' of a ship first. They cut the keel from a long, straight tree trunk. Then they carved two stems and nailed one to either end of the keel. ▼

The fore stem was at the front of the ship.

The keel was the piece of wood along the bottom.

The aft stem was at the back.

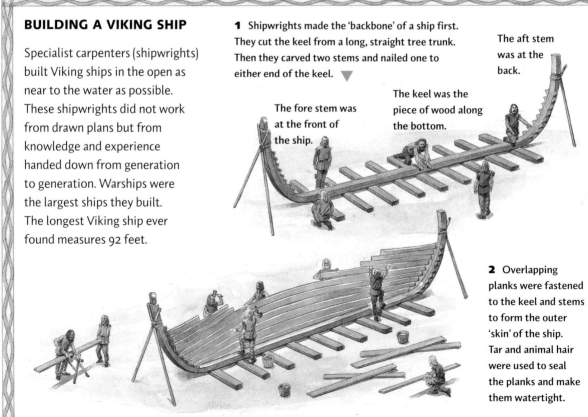

2 Overlapping planks were fastened to the keel and stems to form the outer 'skin' of the ship. Tar and animal hair were used to seal the planks and make them watertight.

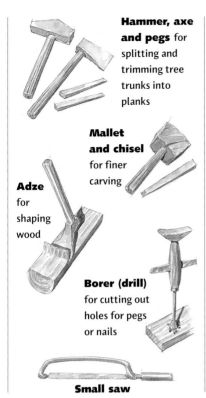

Hammer, axe and pegs for splitting and trimming tree trunks into planks

Mallet and chisel for finer carving

Adze for shaping wood

Borer (drill) for cutting out holes for pegs or nails

Small saw

WOODEN CHURCHES

Wooden-planked churches, called stave churches, were built in Scandinavia to a simple plan. The place where the people stood, the nave, was usually rectangular and the place where the priest conducted the service, the chancel, was square. Four central posts held up the roof. Some churches had aisles and verandas, like this one built in Norway in about 1150. The outside of a stave church was very elaborate. Carvings decorated the ends and edges of the roof and there were often sculptures of animal heads on the uppermost turrets.

Stave churches are called this because their walls were made of wooden staves (planks) set upright in the ground.

3 Inside the ship, cross timbers were added to strengthen the whole structure. ▼

Although warships had sails, they were also propelled by oars – up to fifty on the biggest ships.

4 Finally the prow (front) would be decorated with carvings, and perhaps a dragon's head. ▶

WORDS AND PICTURES

The Vikings had their own form of alphabet. It is called the *futhark,* after the first six characters. The characters or letters are called *runes.* The runes were carved with a sharp point (a knife or a sword) on to wood, stone, bone or metal. Most of the letters are made up of straight lines.

ᚼᚠ : ᛦᛁᛅᚱᛁ :

The name of the Viking craftsman, or the owner, was often put on to precious objects such as brooches. Adventures of warriors and the gods might be carved as picture-stories on to stones. Sometimes the warriors' and the gods' names were carved alongside.

These carved runes say 'Vikings at a glance.' ▶

There were several different versions of the Viking alphabet. This futhark has sixteen characters. ▼

CARVING PICTURES

Viking carvers produced some marvelous pictures.

Carved in wood, this is a picture of two blacksmiths at work. The one on the left is hammering the hot metal, while his assistant is keeping the fire hot with a pair of bellows. ▼

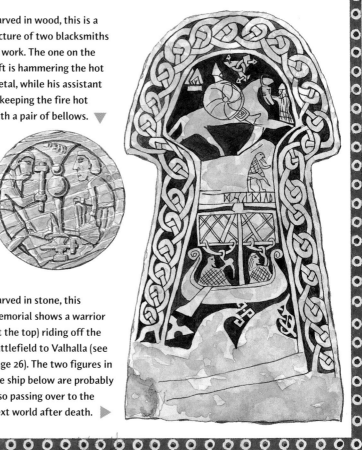

Carved in stone, this memorial shows a warrior (at the top) riding off the battlefield to Valhalla (see page 26). The two figures in the ship below are probably also passing over to the next world after death. ▶

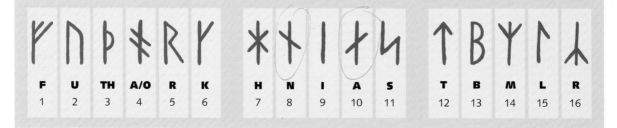

ᚠ	ᚢ	ᚦ	ᚬ	ᚱ	ᚴ	ᚼ	ᚾ	ᛁ	ᛅ	ᛋ	ᛏ	ᛒ	ᛘ	ᛚ	ᛦ
F	U	TH	A/O	R	K	H	N	I	A	S	T	B	M	L	R
1	2	3	4	5	6	7	8	9	10	11	12	13	14	15	16

This case for a comb is made from bone. On one side are runes that read 'kamb: kothan: kiari: Thorfastr', which means 'Thorfast made a good comb.'

SAGAS

The Vikings did not write books but they were great storytellers. Their stories were eventually written down, but not until the main Viking age was over. We can read about some individual Vikings from *sagas*. Sagas are historical novels based on real people and events from the Viking world. Written in the thirteenth century, these family sagas are full of interesting details as well as being good stories.

Njal's Saga is about a blood feud in Iceland around 980. It begins: ▶

There was a man called Mord Fiddle, who was the son of Sighvat the Red. Mord was a powerful chieftain, and lived at Voll in the Rangiver Plains...

Skallagrim and his wife, Bera, finally had another son whom they sprinkled with water and called Egil. As he grew up it soon became obvious that he was going to be as black-haired and ugly as his father. By the time he was three he was as big and strong as a boy of six or seven and wanted to go off on journeys with his father, who said to him, 'You are not going. You don't know how to behave yourself when there is company and a lot of drinking. You are difficult enough to cope with when you're sober.'

Egil's Saga was written in about 1230 by Snorri Sturluson. It is the story of Egil Skallagrimsson – a difficult child who turned out to be a fierce warrior without mercy towards his enemies. ▶

RELIGION

The Vikings believed that there were many gods and goddesses who had power over them and their world. They thought these gods came from two families that had once fought against each other – the Asar and the Vanir. The Vikings worshiped their gods and made sacrifices to them. In return they hoped for good harvests and successful battles.

AFTER DEATH

The Vikings believed that Odin lived in a heavenly place called Asgard in the palace of Valhalla – the great Hall of the Killed. It was here that warriors came after they had been killed in battle. They entered the hall through one of its 640 gates and were welcomed by handmaidens called *Valkyries*. In Valhalla warriors fought and feasted, getting ready for the final world-battle, called the *Ragnarok*, which would bring the world to an end and destroy all the gods.

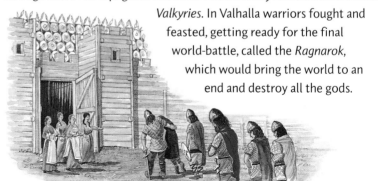

SOME VIKING GODS

Odin was the chief of the gods, the All-father, the god of wisdom and war. He had sacrificed one of his eyes for a drink at the Well of Knowledge. Odin had two ravens, called Hugin (meaning 'mind') and Mugin (meaning 'memory'), who flew the world by day and returned each night to tell the god everything that had happened. Odin is believed to have ridden on a grey, eight-legged horse called Sleipnir.

Frey was the god of fertility.

Frigg was Odin's wife.

Baldr was Odin's son and the god of youth.

Tyr was the god of warriors.

Heimdal was the watchman god.

Thor, the god of thunder, was probably the most popular Viking god. He rode about the sky, fighting evil monsters and giants and killing them with his mighty hammer, Miollnir. Thor's symbol was a hammer and many people wore a hammer pendant around their neck as a lucky charm.

Loki was a troublemaker – a sort of half-god, half-demon. He was the son of a giant and had once been punished by having his lips sewn together, as shown on this stone carving.

VIKING BURIAL

The most usual form of burial for a Viking was in a grave with everything he or she might need for the next world. People were buried with their clothes and some other possessions – tapestries, furniture, carts and looms. Warriors had their weapons, and food and drink for their journey to Valhalla. In addition, their horses, dogs and even slaves might be killed and laid to rest in the same grave. Some rich men and women were buried in ships that would carry them to the next world.

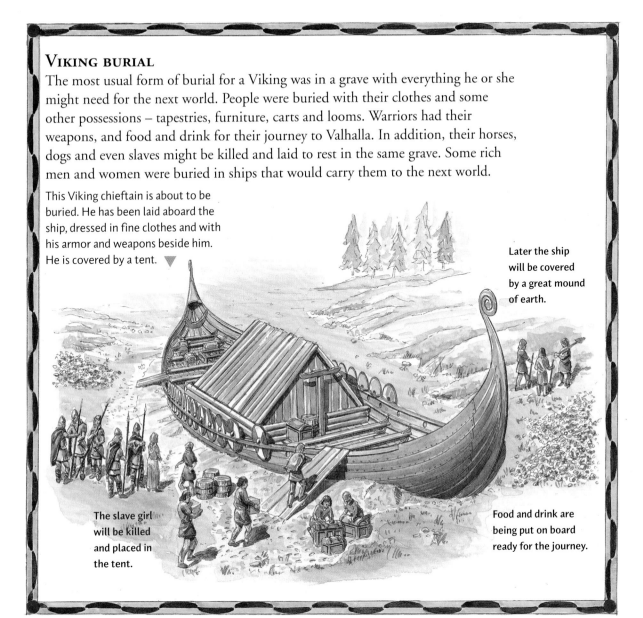

This Viking chieftain is about to be buried. He has been laid aboard the ship, dressed in fine clothes and with his armor and weapons beside him. He is covered by a tent. ▼

Later the ship will be covered by a great mound of earth.

The slave girl will be killed and placed in the tent.

Food and drink are being put on board ready for the journey.

CHRISTIANITY

From the late tenth century the Vikings gradually became Christian, although they often went on worshiping their old gods as well. Denmark was converted by Christian missionaries in the reign of Harald Bluetooth (see page 15).

This is part of a twelfth-century tapestry from a church in Sweden. It shows the old gods, Odin (left), Thor (center) with his hammer, and Frey the fertility god (right) holding an ear of corn.

AFTER THE VIKINGS

By around 1100 the Viking age was really over. But the Viking presence was still felt in the countries that had been raided or occupied. As well as Viking descendants, there were the results of Viking influence on languages, place-names, styles of architecture and decoration. By 1100 Vikings were long settled in places such as Normandy and Britain. At the same time, the Viking homelands were under attack from other invaders.

At the end of the Viking age, warriors began to go into battle on horseback. They were called cavalry. Mounted warriors found that long, pointed shields protected them better than round ones.

ENEMIES OF THE VIKINGS

The Vikings had been feared as the invaders who came across the sea. Now other peoples were beginning to invade the Viking homelands. The Wendish tribes, who lived along the southern shores of the Baltic Sea, had been raiding Scandinavia for nearly 100 years. But by 1100 these raids had become serious. Around Europe kings were beginning to organize their armies and build castles to protect their towns. This meant that they were able to defend themselves from Viking raids.

DESCENDED FROM THE VIKINGS

In 1016 Cnut the Dane became the first Viking to reign over the whole of England. When Cnut died, his son Harthacnut became king. Harthacnut was the last Viking king of England. The Viking king of Norway, Harald Hardrada, later came to claim the English throne but was killed at the Battle of Stamford Bridge in 1066. William the Conqueror, Duke of Normandy, was descended from Rollo the Viking. William's Norman army defeated an English army at the Battle of Hastings in 1066, having crossed the English Channel in ships that still looked Viking.

The Bayeux Tapestry was woven to tell the story of the Norman invasion of England in 1066. The Normans were descended from Vikings who had settled in Normandy, France. ▼

The Bayeux Tapestry shows that William the Conqueror's ship had a prow decorated with a carved animal head and shields along the sides, just like the ships sailed by William's Viking ancestors (see page 22). ▶

HORNED HELMETS

Pictures drawn in modern times often show Vikings with horned helmets, but that is wrong. Only the helmets that appear in carvings and in stories from Viking mythology had horns. Look back to page 20 to see what *real* Viking helmets looked like.

Look back to page 20 to see what *real* Viking helmets looked like.

THE LAST YEARS OF THE VIKINGS

c.1000 Vikings reach North America

1014 Vikings are defeated by Brian Boru, the king of the Irish

1035 Harthacnut becomes the last Viking king of England

1066 Norwegian Vikings defeated by the English at the Battle of Stamford Bridge

1066 William Duke of Normandy, descended from Rollo the Viking, defeats the English at the Battle of Hastings

1107 Norwegian king leads a crusade to Jerusalem

1241 Swedes now rule Finland

1263 Iceland and Greenland are occupied by Norway

1341 The Inuit begin to occupy Greenland

1400s Last Norwegian colony in Greenland

The Inuit are thought to have traveled from Canada to settle in Greenland.

VIKING INFLUENCE

Stone carvers working in Britain in the Norman period were influenced by designs and ideas that had been introduced by the Vikings. At this twelfth-century church at Kilpeck, in southwest England, you can still see Viking styles of decoration today.

These carvings around the door of Kilpeck church feature designs of twisting snakes and scroll patterns in the Viking style.

VIKING WORDS

There are still Viking names and words in the English language to show that the Vikings occupied parts of Britain.

Place-names ending with:
'-kirk' come from *kirkja* (church);
'-ness' come from *nes* (headland).

Names of places ending with:
'-wick' were market places;
'-by' were villages;
'-haven' were harbors.

Some Viking words are still used in English, for example:
'fell' from the word *fjall* (a hill);
'beck' from the word *bekkr* (a stream).

One in five of the everyday words used in English today was introduced by the Vikings. These include: leg, sky, white, skin, egg, low, root, skirt, knife, ugly, ill, window and husband.

GLOSSARY

Althing An assembly (*thing*) of all the freemen of Iceland

Fort A place for warriors and their families to live which was heavily defended by banks of earth and timber

Hneftafl A board game where one player had eight pieces to protect the king from another player using sixteen pieces

Jarl A chieftain, the highest rank of Viking noble below the king

Karlars Free Vikings ruled by *jarls*

Keel The large piece of wood that runs along the bottom of a ship or boat

Knarr A type of ship used by Viking traders and settlers

Monastery The place where communities of monks or nuns lived

Nithing A Viking who had disobeyed the law and so had to give up his possessions and leave his country

Quern A stone for grinding grain into flour for bread

Ragnarok The final battle which the Vikings believed would bring the world to an end

Runes The characters or letters of the Viking alphabet (*futhark*)

Sagas Stories of Viking kings and heroes based on real people and events

Skald A travelling poet

Spindle A wooden rod that has a round weight (whorl) attached to it and is used to spin wool or flax into thread

Stave church A church made from wooden planks (staves)

Thing A district assembly of free Vikings

Thrall A slave who could be bought and sold

Valhalla The place where Vikings hoped to go when they died

Valkyries Female helpers who welcomed Viking warriors to Valhalla

Wergild A fine paid as a penalty for killing someone

INDEX